GOAL OF THE GAME

Written by Kat and Keaton Parks
Illustrated by Dacil Curbelos

To our sweet Cilly boy

In a bustling town with a soccer field so grand,
Lived CJ Striker, with a ball in his hand.

Winning the championship had always been his dream,
But he knew he'd need the help of his team.
The game was tonight, nerves starting to brew,
But CJ knew his team could pull through.

CJ was hopeful, with a smile so bright,
He'd thought of this game all morning and night.
Coach Grant approached and said with a glance,
"CJ, we'll need your help to advance!
Keep your mind sharp and your vision clear,
Look for the shot when the goal draws near!"
BULLDOGS
BULLDOGS

CJ beamed and said with delight,
"I'll help us all shine so brilliantly bright!
Together we're strong, together we'll thrive!
Hands in, everyone—it's victory time!"

But Jack Kickwell, with a flair for the ball,
Liked to take shots, never passing at all.
Though quick and skillful with his aim,
He often forgot that teamwork wins the game.
BULLDOGS US TIGER
TIME
45:00

They headed out onto the field,
but CJ just knew,
If Jack could be a team player,
their dreams would come true.

The game began with a fierce, lively cheer,
The moment they've waited for was finally here.

CJ encouraged his team and said,
"When you get the ball, just pick up your head.
If you don't see a shot, then pass the ball,
This is our game, we've got this y'all!"

Jack charged with the ball, oh so fast,
But a defender was there, and he couldn't get past.
CJ saw Jack's trouble and shouted with glee,
"Pass it, Jack, I'm open! I'm free!"

Jack paused for a second—he wanted the fame.
"Leave it to me, I can win us this game."

Jack tried to shoot, but the ball was blocked.
The game was still tied, and the clock tick-tocked.
BULLDOGS

BULLDOGS VS TIGERS
TIME
08:13
0
0
CJ thought hard and gave Jack a clue: "Remember, your team is here to help you!"
BULLDOGS
BULLDOGS

The game went on, the Tigers getting close.
They aimed for the goal, but instead hit the post.

Both teams tried their best, but neither could score,
Coach Grant was sure that they would fight more!

Jack had the ball again—this was his shot.
But this time, he stopped, and gave it a thought.
He spotted CJ in an open position,
So he passed the ball to him with precision.

CJ received it and scanned the field,
But instead of shooting, another chance revealed!
He saw that Jack was open and near,
So CJ passed the ball back to his peer.
BULLDOGS VS TIGERS
TIME
00:10
BULLDOGS
BULLDOGS

Jack took the shot with a powerful kick,
The ball soared high, and the crowd rose quick.

The net swished, and the game was done—
The Bulldogs beat the Tigers by one!

Jack looked amazed and said, "Why not?
Why wouldn't you take the game-winning shot?"
CJ smiled and shrugged, saying with ease,
"Winning together is what matters to me."

BULLDOGS VS TIGERS
1 TIME 0
00:00

BULLDOGS

Coach Grant smiled and gave CJ a high-five,
"We couldn't have done it without your steady eye."
But CJ knew he only played a small part.
"We wouldn't have won without team effort and heart!"

Jack learned a lesson that he'd never forget—
Winning together is better, you bet!
Scoring is nice, but what's even greater,
Is winning as a team, not just as a player.

So remember this story, and you will see—
The goal of the game is to work as a team.

The End.

About the Authors

Kat and Keaton Parks were inspired to write Goal of the Game by their one-year-old son's love of books and story time. Keaton, a professional soccer player for New York City FC, brings his passion for the sport into the story, while Kat adds her creative touch to craft a fun and engaging tale that celebrates the joy of soccer, teamwork, and friendly competition.